A Mother's Love Is Made Up Of . . .

by Cyrano De Words-u-lac

A Mother's Love Is Made Up Of . . .
ISBN 0-88144-179-1
Copyright © 1996 Dan & Dave Davidson
Rhymeo Ink
P.O. Box 1416
Salem, Virginia 24153

Application has been made for a registered federal trademark for "Rhymeo" and "Show-It Poet."

Published by Trade Life
P.O. Box 55325
Tulsa, Oklahoma 74155

WHAT'S A RHYMEO™?

Rhymeos™ are fat-free un-poetry — lite and lean literary cuisine. Rhymeos™ are short and sketchy, quick and catchy — two short lines reinforced in rhyme. Although the short rhyming couplets display a poetic flavor, they are not traditional poetry. They are actually jingles about life — Jingle Verse Poetry for the 21st Century — offering insight and motivation, humor and inspiration.

Cyrano De Words-u-lac pens the shortest verse in the universe — a story to tell in a nutshell, a rhyming report to make a long story short. Rhymeos™ are short and sweet and poetically petite — clever ways to paraphrase — bite-sized words to the wise. Whether concise advice or an easy doesy fuzzy wuzzy, Rhymeos™ give a reflective perspective in a fireside chat format. It's literary rap with a snap — poetically correct dialect — a way to cope with humor and hope!

dedicated with love
to our wives Kim and Joan
and the other special mothers in
our lives — Darlene, Diane, Myrt and Elaine

Celebrating The Good In Motherhood

There's something in my heart no one can take away,
a sacrifice of love I won't be able to repay.

With memories of my mother, one day I was inspired
to reflect on her devotion and all that I admired.

I began with pen in hand to describe a mother's love,
a recipe from Cyrano of what moms are made of.

It became a Rhymeo™ celebration of all that's good,
a collection of treasures found in motherhood.

Cyrano De Words-u-lac

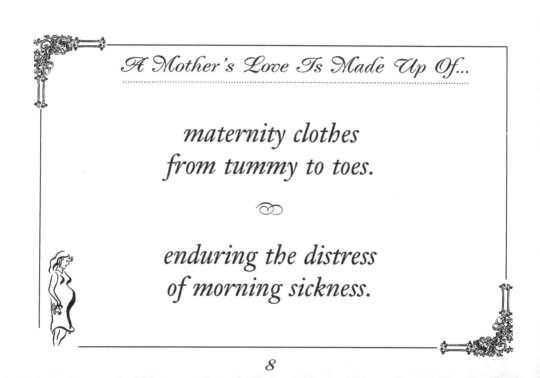

A Mother's Love Is Made Up Of...

maternity clothes
from tummy to toes.

∽

enduring the distress
of morning sickness.

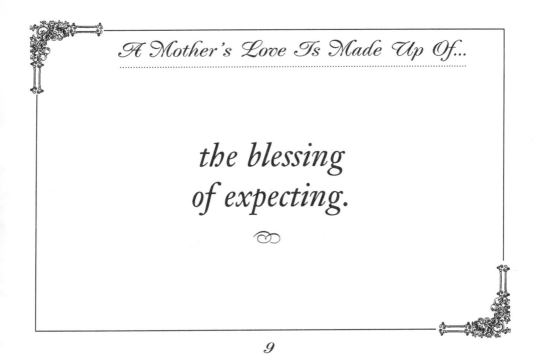

A Mother's Love Is Made Up Of...

*the blessing
of expecting.*

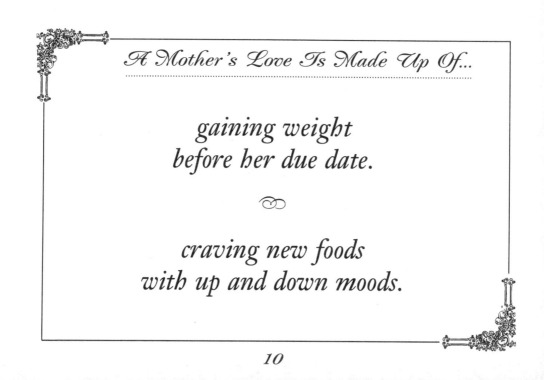

A Mother's Love Is Made Up Of...

gaining weight
before her due date.

∞

craving new foods
with up and down moods.

A Mother's Love Is Made Up Of...

new baby showers,
spring wild flowers.

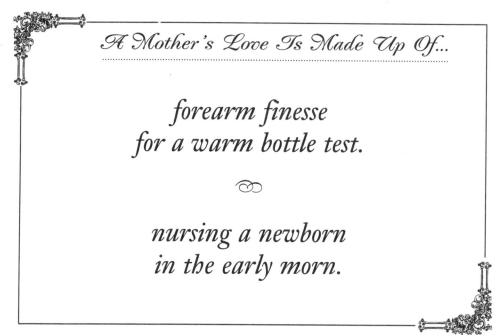

A Mother's Love Is Made Up Of...

forearm finesse
for a warm bottle test.

∞

nursing a newborn
in the early morn.

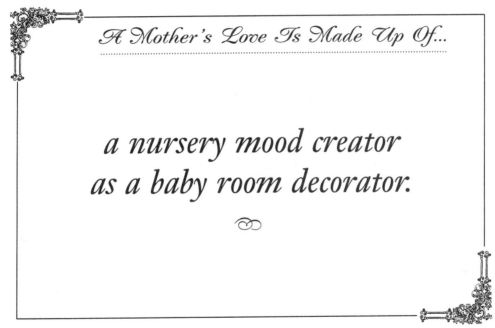

A Mother's Love Is Made Up Of...

*a nursery mood creator
as a baby room decorator.*

A Mother's Love Is Made Up Of...

*a late night feed
for a baby in need.*

∞

*a pacifier
purifier.*

A Mother's Love Is Made Up Of...

a teddy bear,
a daily prayer.

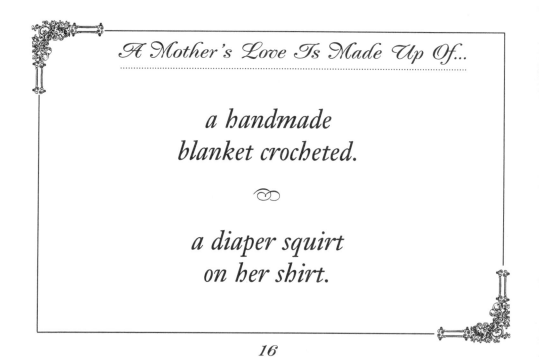

A Mother's Love Is Made Up Of...

*a handmade
blanket crocheted.*

*a diaper squirt
on her shirt.*

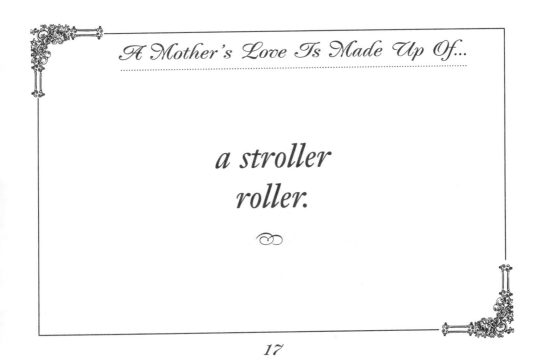

A Mother's Love Is Made Up Of...

*a stroller
roller.*

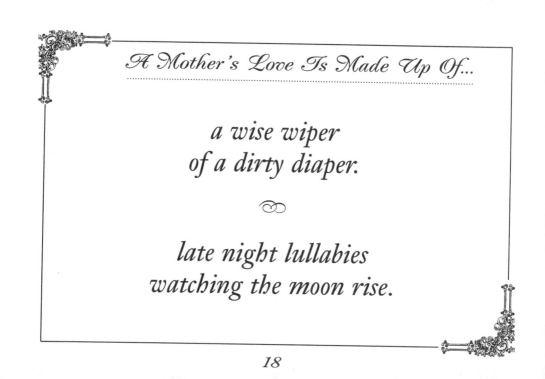

A Mother's Love Is Made Up Of...

a wise wiper
of a dirty diaper.

∞

late night lullabies
watching the moon rise.

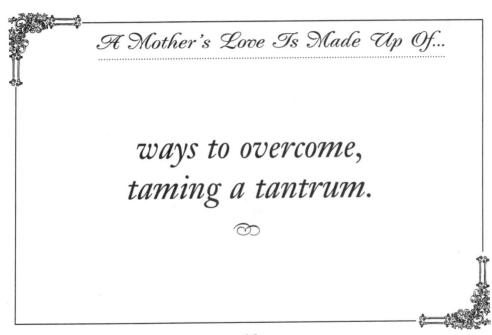

*ways to overcome,
taming a tantrum.*

A Mother's Love Is Made Up Of...

toddler weaning
and snack screening.

a stocked diaper bag,
a bargain price tag.

*adjusting highchairs
and gates for stairs.*

A Mother's Love Is Made Up Of...

toddler time outs
for playground pouts.

chasing butterflies
under blue skies.

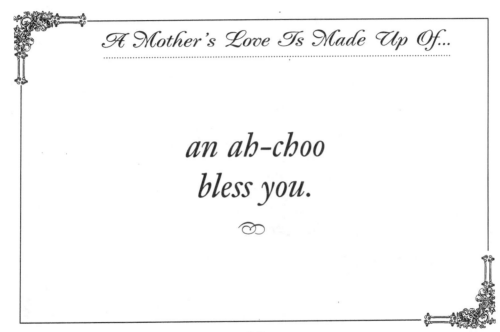

A Mother's Love Is Made Up Of...

an ah-choo
bless you.

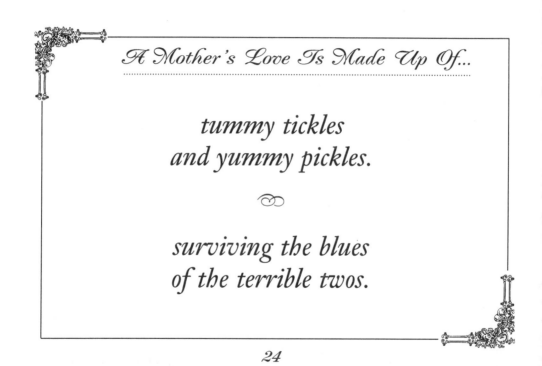

A Mother's Love Is Made Up Of...

tummy tickles
and yummy pickles.

surviving the blues
of the terrible twos.

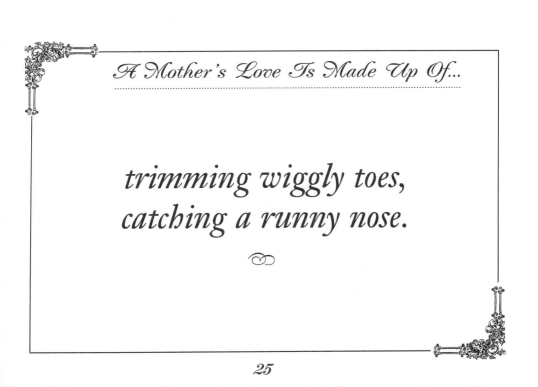

A Mother's Love Is Made Up Of...

*trimming wiggly toes,
catching a runny nose.*

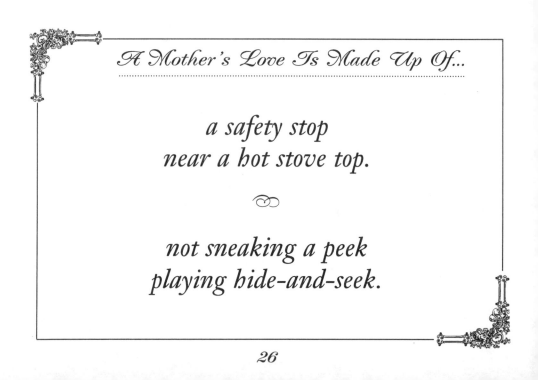

A Mother's Love Is Made Up Of...

a safety stop
near a hot stove top.

∞

not sneaking a peek
playing hide-and-seek.

A Mother's Love Is Made Up Of...

*checking late at night
for kids tucked in tight.*

A Mother's Love Is Made Up Of...

*knowing what to do
for a fever or flu.*

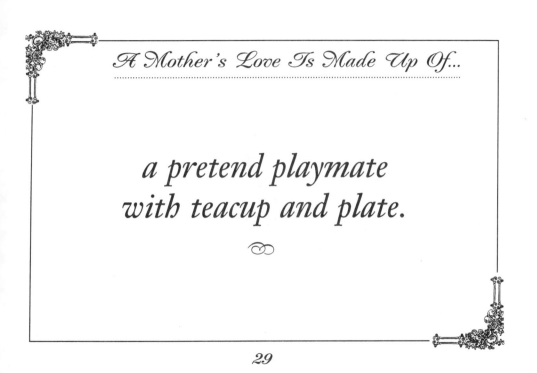

A Mother's Love Is Made Up Of...

*a pretend playmate
with teacup and plate.*

A Mother's Love Is Made Up Of...

*treats in the car
when traveling far.*

*cleaning dirty underwear,
washing the potty chair.*

A Mother's Love Is Made Up Of...

a breakfast bib,
a pardoned fib.

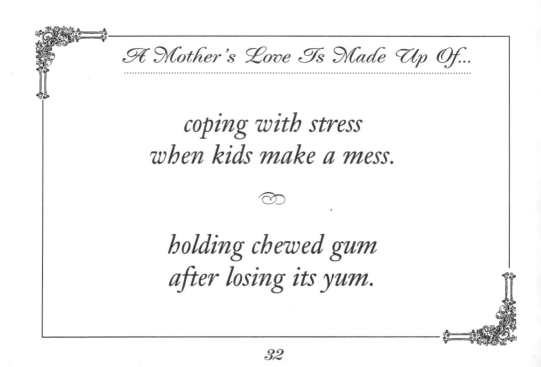

A Mother's Love Is Made Up Of...

coping with stress
when kids make a mess.

holding chewed gum
after losing its yum.

A Mother's Love Is Made Up Of...

*singing ABC's
and counting 123's.*

A Mother's Love Is Made Up Of...

*a healthy holdout
for a Brussels sprout.*

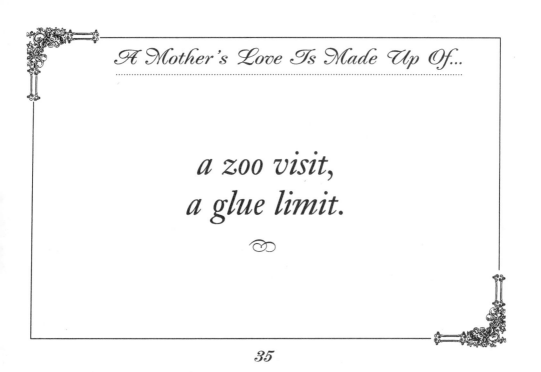

A Mother's Love Is Made Up Of...

a zoo visit,
a glue limit.

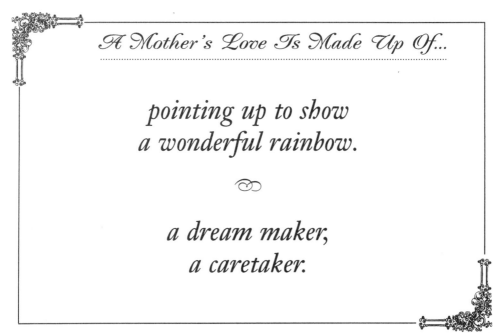

A Mother's Love Is Made Up Of...

*pointing up to show
a wonderful rainbow.*

*a dream maker,
a caretaker.*

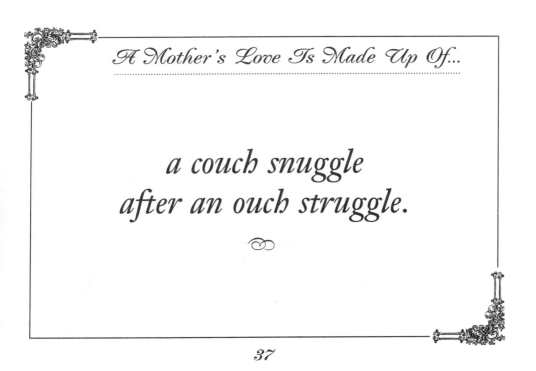

A Mother's Love Is Made Up Of...

a couch snuggle
after an ouch struggle.

A Mother's Love Is Made Up Of...

a cookie jar,
a wishing star.

not complaining
after finger painting.

A Mother's Love Is Made Up Of...

*a mandatory
bedtime story.*

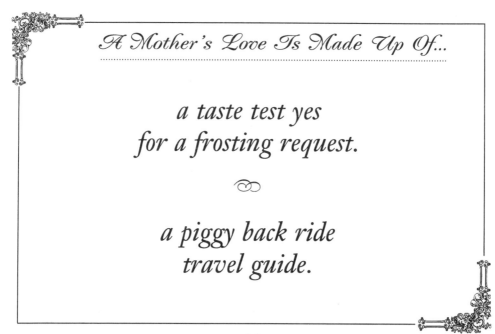

A Mother's Love Is Made Up Of...

*a taste test yes
for a frosting request.*

∞

*a piggy back ride
travel guide.*

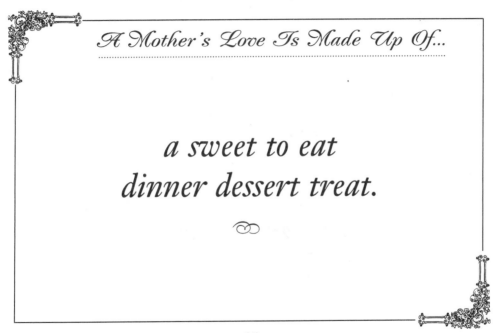

A Mother's Love Is Made Up Of...

*a sweet to eat
dinner dessert treat.*

A Mother's Love Is Made Up Of...

a bathroom blush
when kids forget to flush.

∞

playing with baby blocks,
caring for chickenpox.

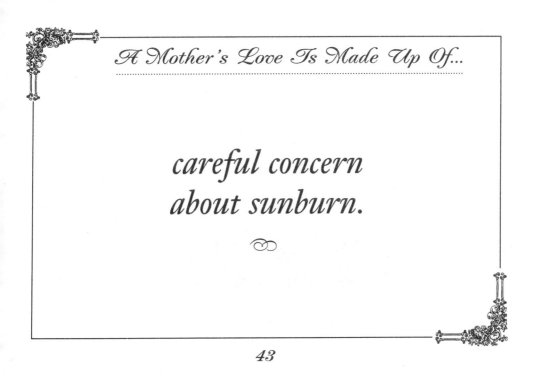

A Mother's Love Is Made Up Of...

careful concern
about sunburn.

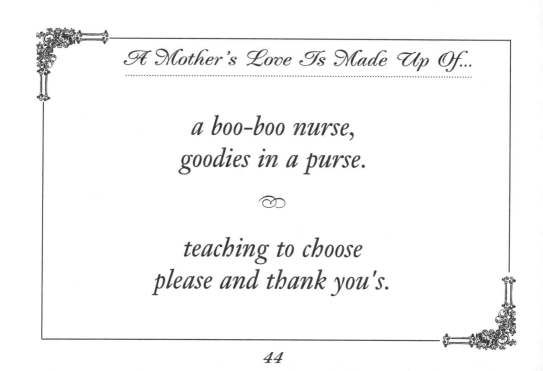

A Mother's Love Is Made Up Of...

a boo-boo nurse,
goodies in a purse.

teaching to choose
please and thank you's.

A Mother's Love Is Made Up Of...

*a nursery rhyme
before bedtime.*

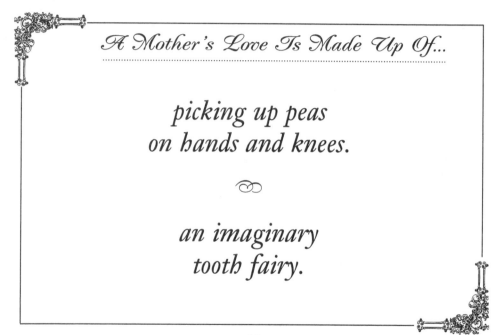

A Mother's Love Is Made Up Of...

*picking up peas
on hands and knees.*

∞

*an imaginary
tooth fairy.*

A Mother's Love Is Made Up Of...

*keeping kids clean
with healthy hygiene.*

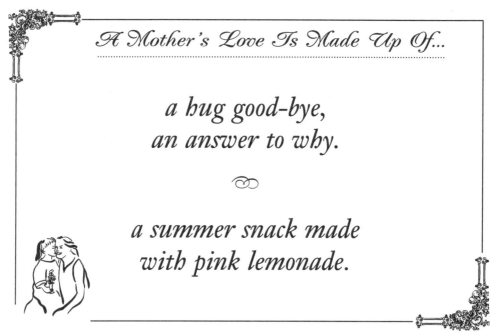

A Mother's Love Is Made Up Of...

a hug good-bye,
an answer to why.

∞

a summer snack made
with pink lemonade.

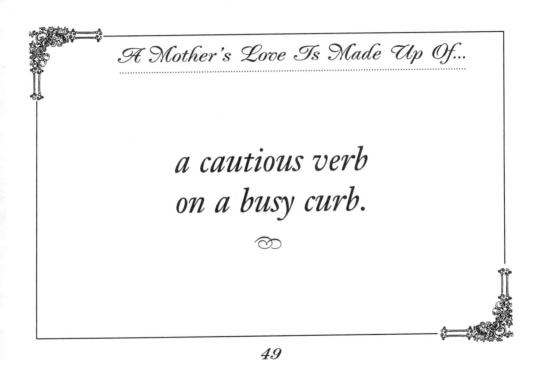

*a cautious verb
on a busy curb.*

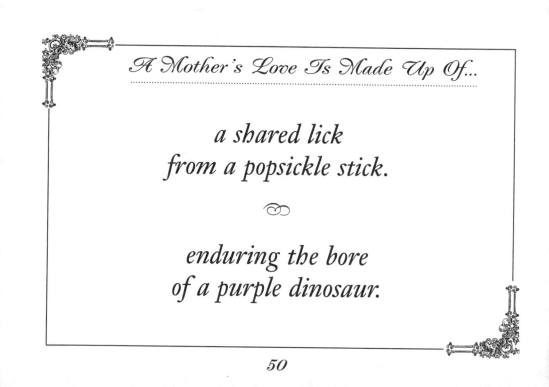

A Mother's Love Is Made Up Of...

a shared lick
from a popsickle stick.

enduring the bore
of a purple dinosaur.

*a hulahooper
happy trooper.*

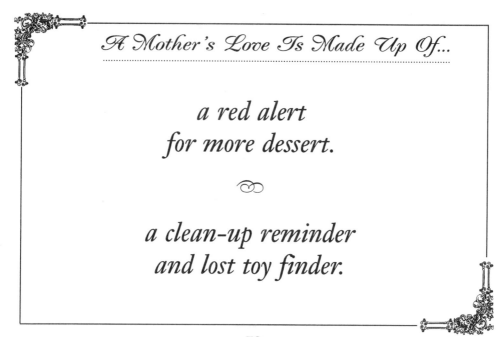

A Mother's Love Is Made Up Of...

a red alert
for more dessert.

a clean-up reminder
and lost toy finder.

A Mother's Love Is Made Up Of...

midnight snacks
for insomniacs.

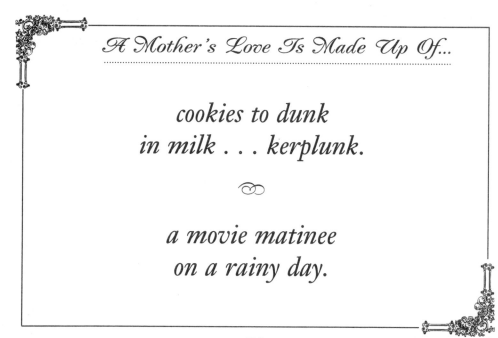

A Mother's Love Is Made Up Of...

cookies to dunk
in milk . . . kerplunk.

a movie matinee
on a rainy day.

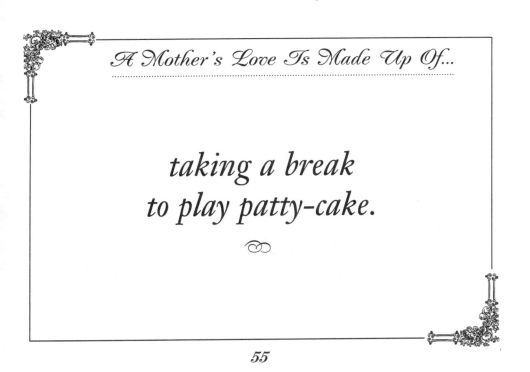

A Mother's Love Is Made Up Of...

*taking a break
to play patty-cake.*

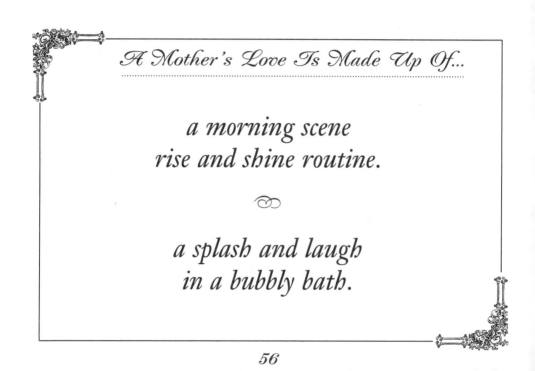

A Mother's Love Is Made Up Of...

a morning scene
rise and shine routine.

a splash and laugh
in a bubbly bath.

A Mother's Love Is Made Up Of...

*playing at the park
right up until dark.*

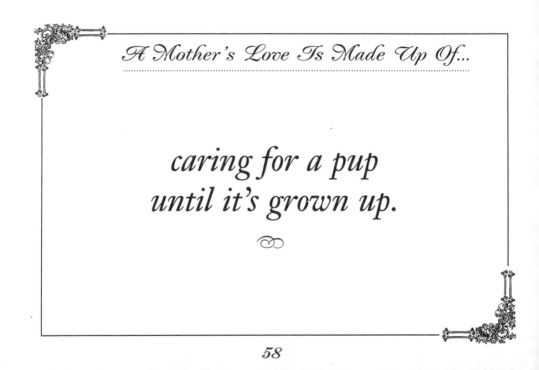

*caring for a pup
until it's grown up.*

A Mother's Love Is Made Up Of...

*fixing favorite meals,
watching kid cartwheels.*

*a forgiven lie
for a false alibi.*

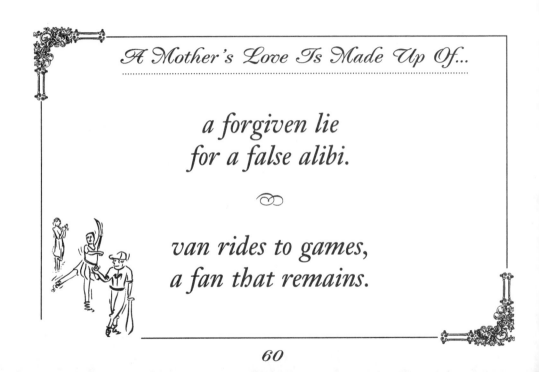

*van rides to games,
a fan that remains.*

A Mother's Love Is Made Up Of...

*make believe
magic up her sleeve.*

A Mother's Love Is Made Up Of...

*helping to fly
a kite in the sky.*

*taming the twitches
of getting stitches.*

*cooking to please
with macaroni and cheese.*

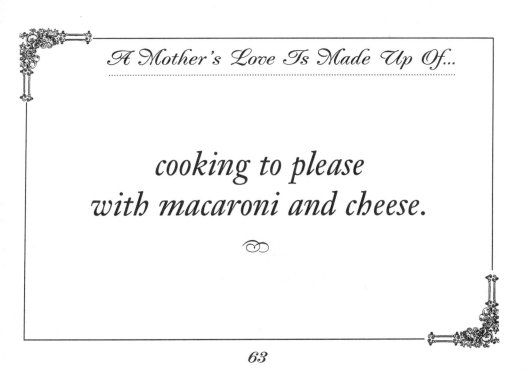

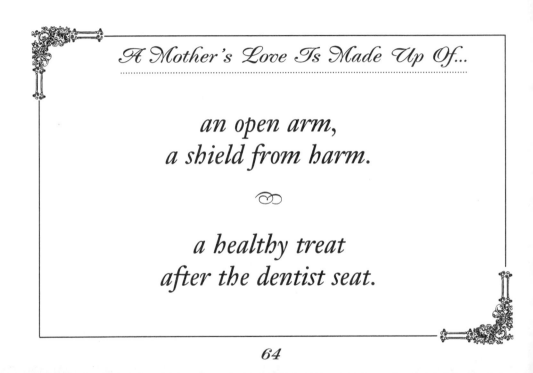

A Mother's Love Is Made Up Of...

an open arm,
a shield from harm.

∞

a healthy treat
after the dentist seat.

A Mother's Love Is Made Up Of...

*a best buddy
when muddy.*

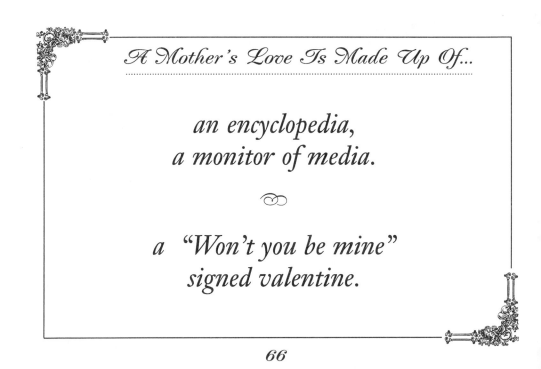

A Mother's Love Is Made Up Of...

an encyclopedia,
a monitor of media.

a *"Won't you be mine"*
signed valentine.

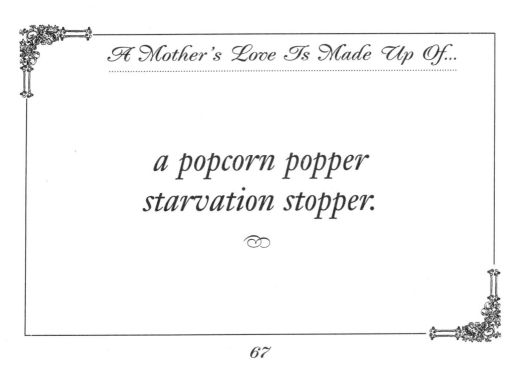

A Mother's Love Is Made Up Of...

*a popcorn popper
starvation stopper.*

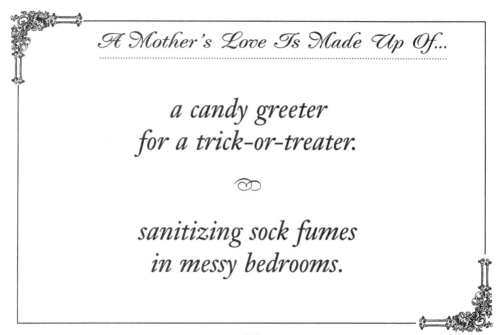

A Mother's Love Is Made Up Of...

a candy greeter
for a trick-or-treater.

∞

sanitizing sock fumes
in messy bedrooms.

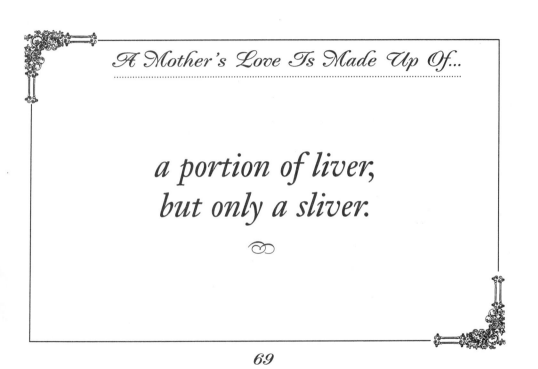

A Mother's Love Is Made Up Of...

*a portion of liver,
but only a sliver.*

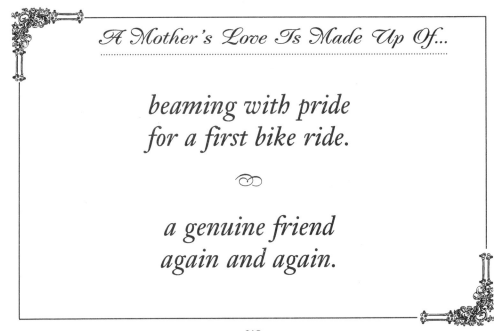

A Mother's Love Is Made Up Of...

beaming with pride
for a first bike ride.

a genuine friend
again and again.

A Mother's Love Is Made Up Of...

a laundry folder,
a welcome shoulder.

*a problem solver,
an errand revolver.*

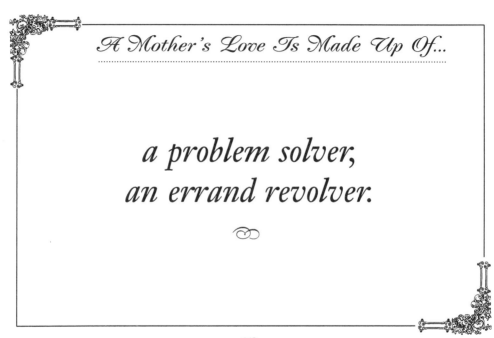

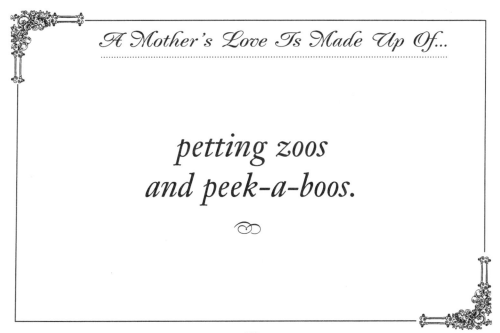

A Mother's Love Is Made Up Of...

*petting zoos
and peek-a-boos.*

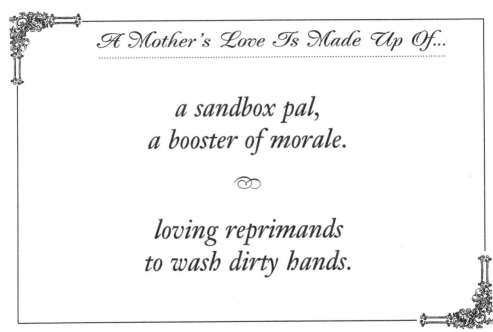

A Mother's Love Is Made Up Of...

a sandbox pal,
a booster of morale.

loving reprimands
to wash dirty hands.

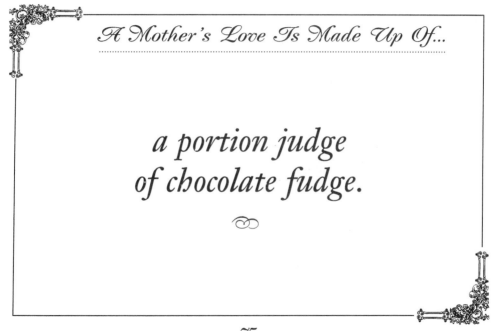

A Mother's Love Is Made Up Of...

*a portion judge
of chocolate fudge.*

A Mother's Love Is Made Up Of...

*washing behind ears
while juggling careers.*

A Mother's Love Is Made Up Of...

keeping kids fed
on home-made bread.

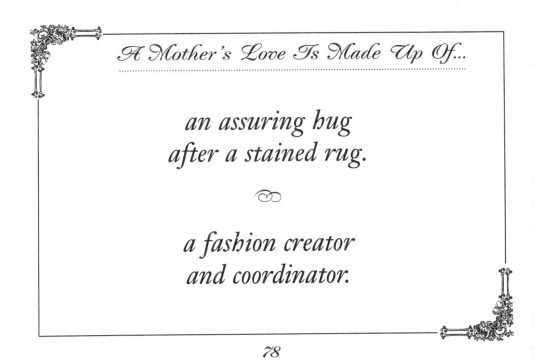

A Mother's Love Is Made Up Of...

an assuring hug
after a stained rug.

a fashion creator
and coordinator.

*a balloon blower
and a party thrower.*

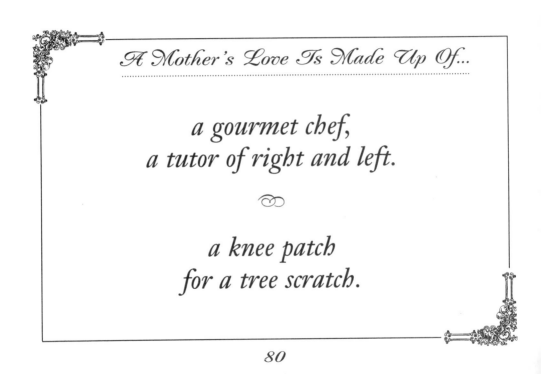

A Mother's Love Is Made Up Of...

a gourmet chef,
a tutor of right and left.

a knee patch
for a tree scratch.

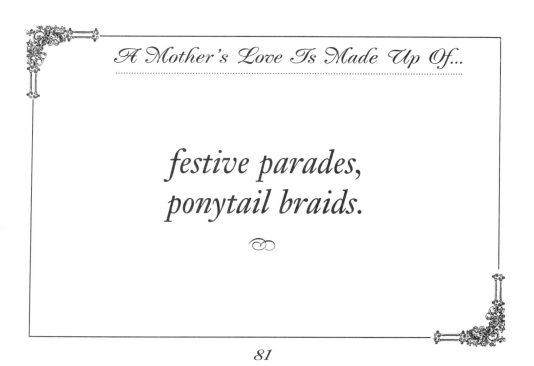

A Mother's Love Is Made Up Of...

*festive parades,
ponytail braids.*

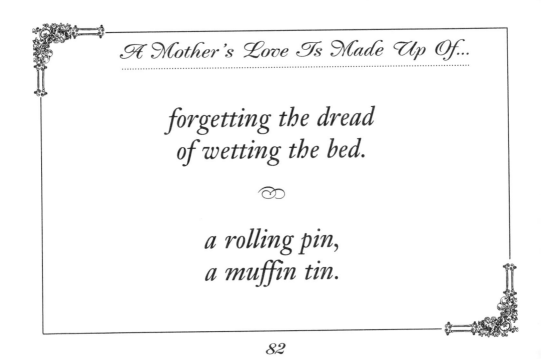

*forgetting the dread
of wetting the bed.*

*a rolling pin,
a muffin tin.*

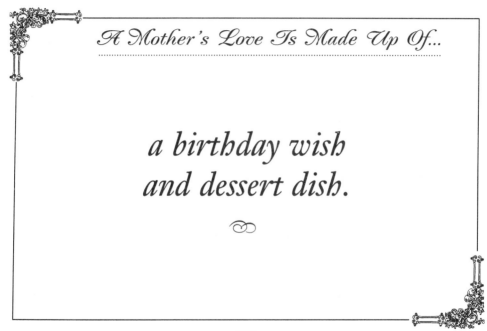

A Mother's Love Is Made Up Of...

a birthday wish
and dessert dish.

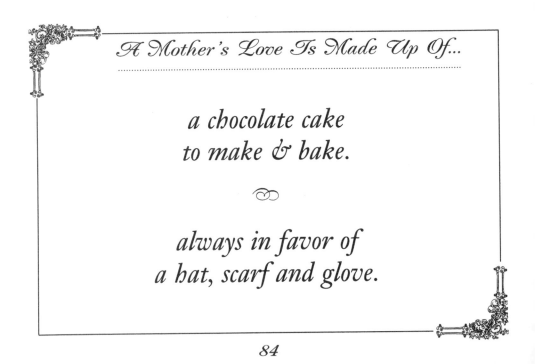

A Mother's Love Is Made Up Of...

*a chocolate cake
to make & bake.*

∞

*always in favor of
a hat, scarf and glove.*

*county fair tries
at baking apple pies.*

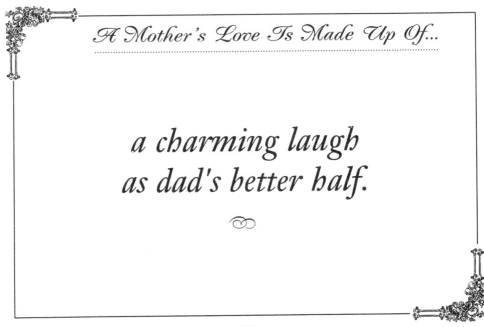

A Mother's Love Is Made Up Of...

*a charming laugh
as dad's better half.*

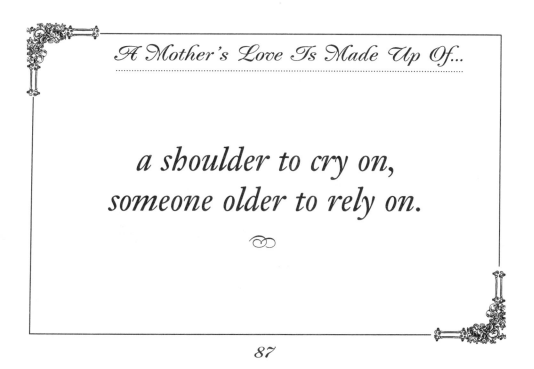

A Mother's Love Is Made Up Of...

a shoulder to cry on,
someone older to rely on.

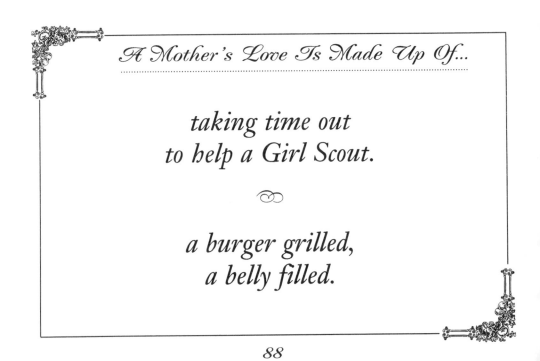

A Mother's Love Is Made Up Of...

taking time out
to help a Girl Scout.

a burger grilled,
a belly filled.

a hand-me-down,
a merry-go-round.

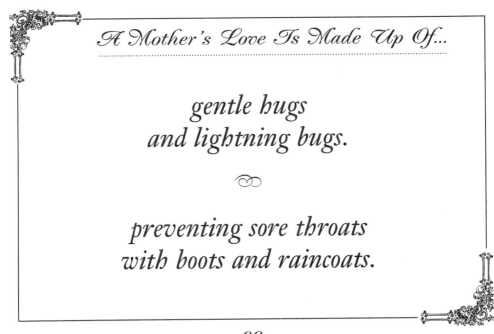

A Mother's Love Is Made Up Of...

gentle hugs
and lightning bugs.

∞

preventing sore throats
with boots and raincoats.

A Mother's Love Is Made Up Of...

wiping away tears,
calming childhood fears.

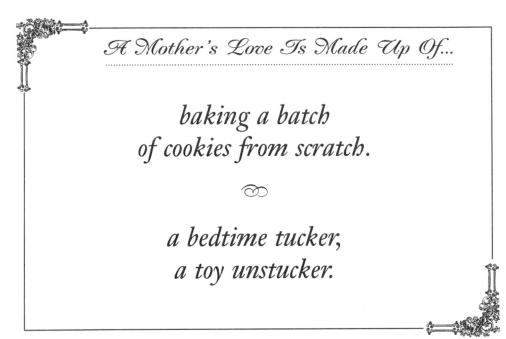

A Mother's Love Is Made Up Of...

baking a batch
of cookies from scratch.

a bedtime tucker,
a toy unstucker.

A Mother's Love Is Made Up Of...

never quitting
at baby sitting.

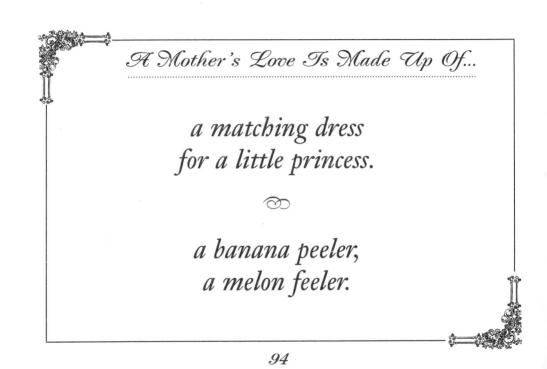

A Mother's Love Is Made Up Of...

a matching dress
for a little princess.

∞

a banana peeler,
a melon feeler.

A Mother's Love Is Made Up Of...

*safety rules
for swimming pools.*

*the golden rule
example for school.*

A Mother's Love Is Made Up Of...

having patience when drinks are spilled again.

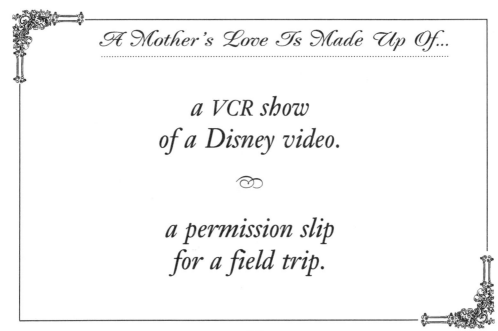

A Mother's Love Is Made Up Of...

*a VCR show
of a Disney video.*

∞

*a permission slip
for a field trip.*

A Mother's Love Is Made Up Of...

*an after school snack
when the bus comes back.*

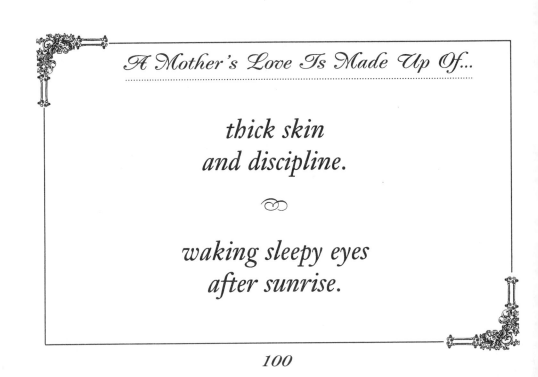

A Mother's Love Is Made Up Of...

*thick skin
and discipline.*

∞

*waking sleepy eyes
after sunrise.*

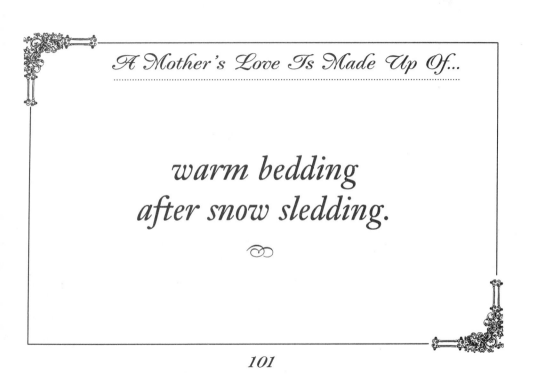

A Mother's Love Is Made Up Of...

*warm bedding
after snow sledding.*

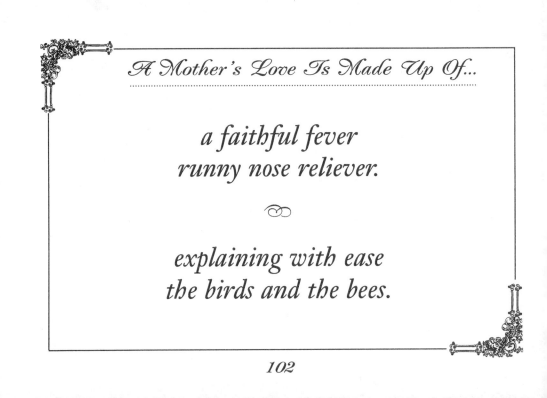

A Mother's Love Is Made Up Of...

*a faithful fever
runny nose reliever.*

*explaining with ease
the birds and the bees.*

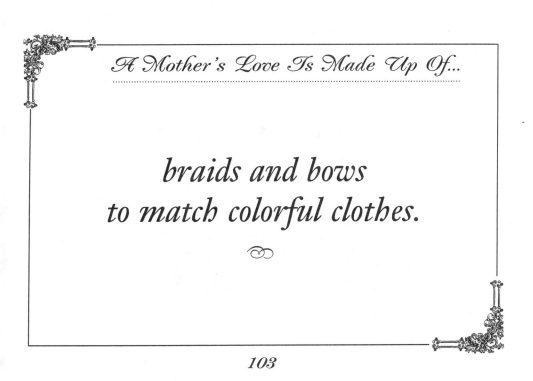

A Mother's Love Is Made Up Of...

*braids and bows
to match colorful clothes.*

A Mother's Love Is Made Up Of...

family fun
when work is done.

∞

a lunch box surprise
to munch on fruit pies.

*a dish washer
and clothes tosser.*

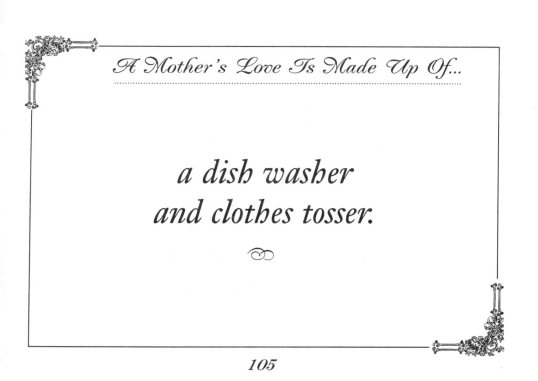

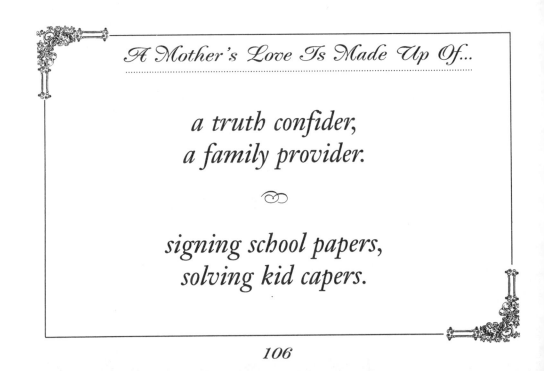

A Mother's Love Is Made Up Of...

a truth confider,
a family provider.

signing school papers,
solving kid capers.

*a savory smell
at the dinner bell.*

*finding good buys
on school supplies.*

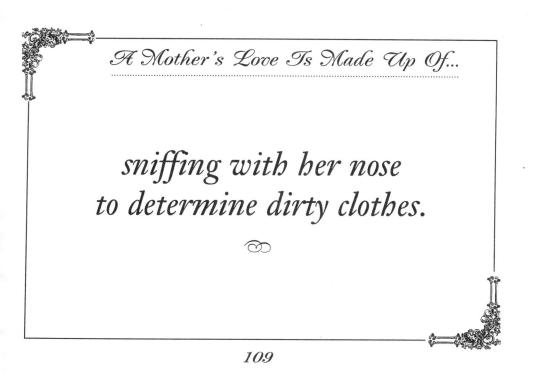

A Mother's Love Is Made Up Of...

*sniffing with her nose
to determine dirty clothes.*

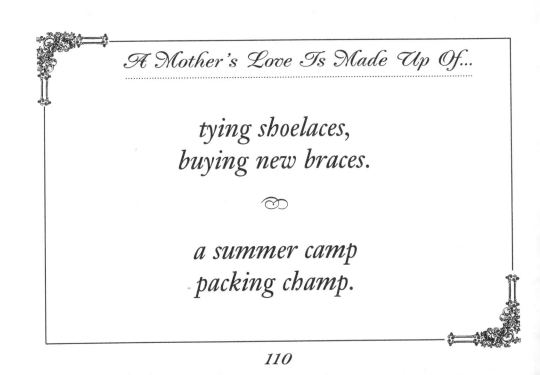

A Mother's Love Is Made Up Of...

*tying shoelaces,
buying new braces.*

*a summer camp
packing champ.*

A Mother's Love Is Made Up Of...

a laundry aid,
a loving maid.

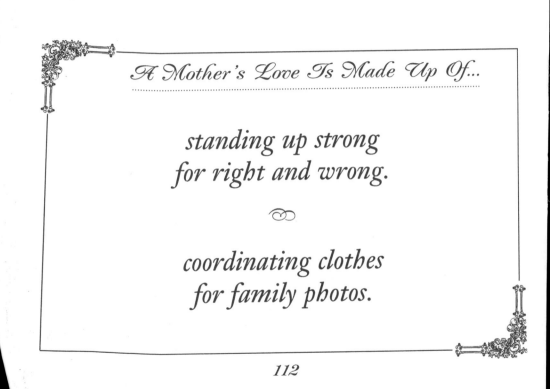

A Mother's Love Is Made Up Of...

standing up strong
for right and wrong.

coordinating clothes
for family photos.

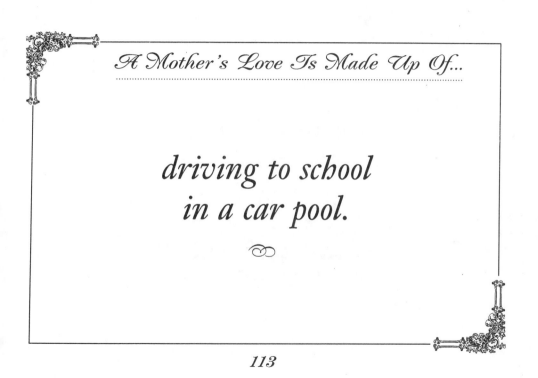

A Mother's Love Is Made Up Of...

driving to school
in a car pool.

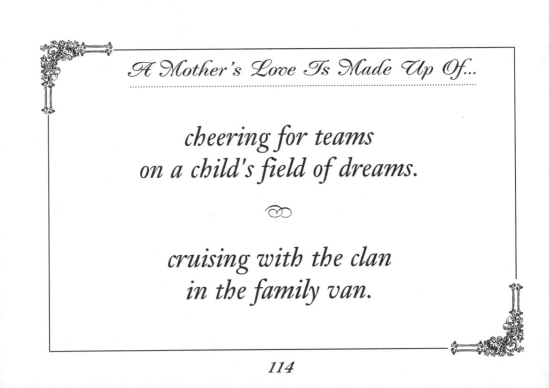

A Mother's Love Is Made Up Of...

*cheering for teams
on a child's field of dreams.*

∞

*cruising with the clan
in the family van.*

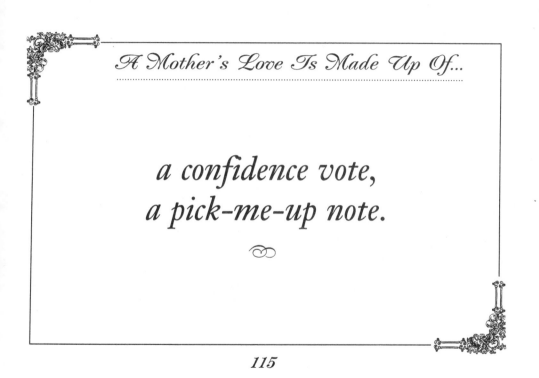

A Mother's Love Is Made Up Of...

a confidence vote,
a pick-me-up note.

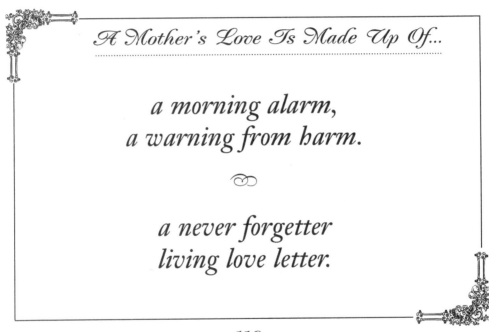

A Mother's Love Is Made Up Of...

a morning alarm,
a warning from harm.

a never forgetter
living love letter.

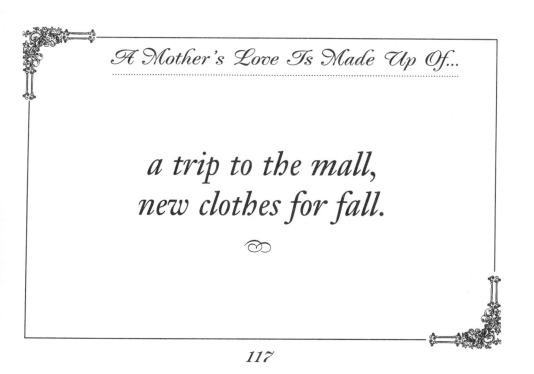

A Mother's Love Is Made Up Of...

*a trip to the mall,
new clothes for fall.*

A Mother's Love Is Made Up Of...

a listening ear,
kind and sincere.

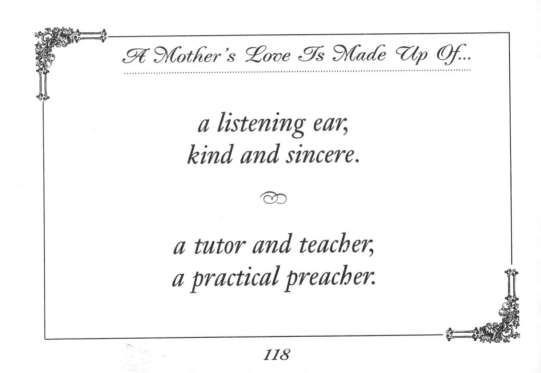

a tutor and teacher,
a practical preacher.

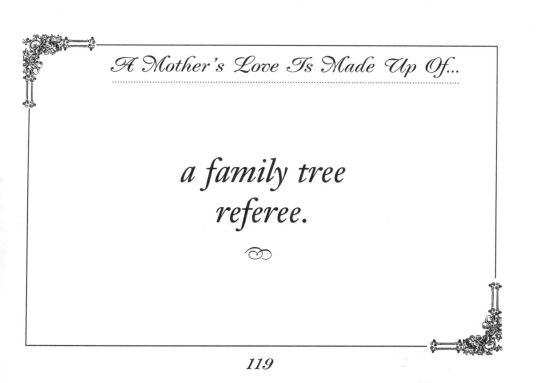

A Mother's Love Is Made Up Of...

*a family tree
referee.*

A Mother's Love Is Made Up Of...

*tolerating a fad
without getting mad.*

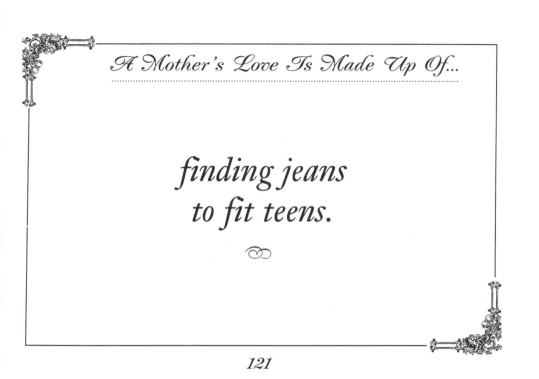

*finding jeans
to fit teens.*

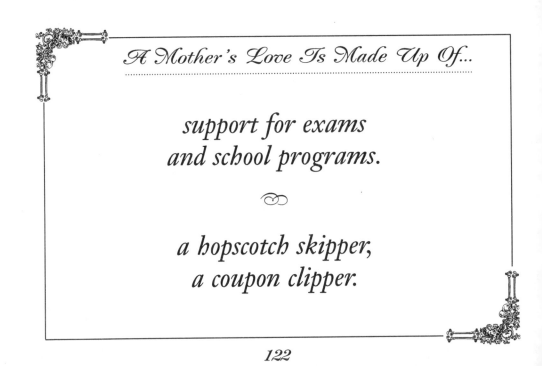

A Mother's Love Is Made Up Of...

support for exams
and school programs.

a hopscotch skipper,
a coupon clipper.

A Mother's Love Is Made Up Of...

back-to-school clothes,
new shoes for growing toes.

A Mother's Love Is Made Up Of...

a schedule planner,
a reminder of manners.

not having a short fuse
over report card news.

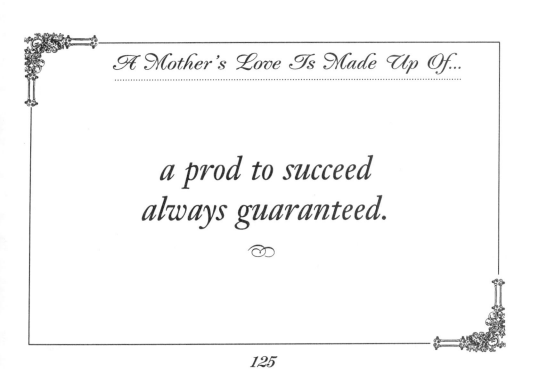

A Mother's Love Is Made Up Of...

a prod to succeed
always guaranteed.

A Mother's Love Is Made Up Of...

*a homework helper,
an anxiety melter.*

*hip hip hurrahs
and beating the blahs.*

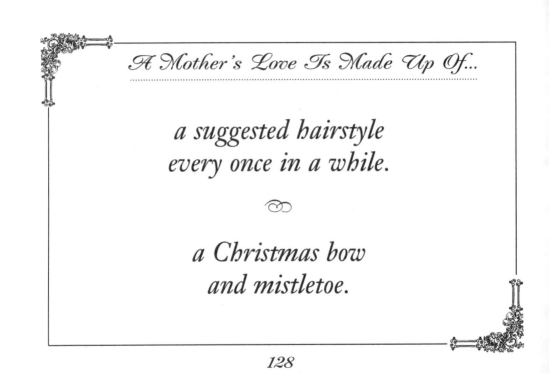

A Mother's Love Is Made Up Of...

*a suggested hairstyle
every once in a while.*

*a Christmas bow
and mistletoe.*

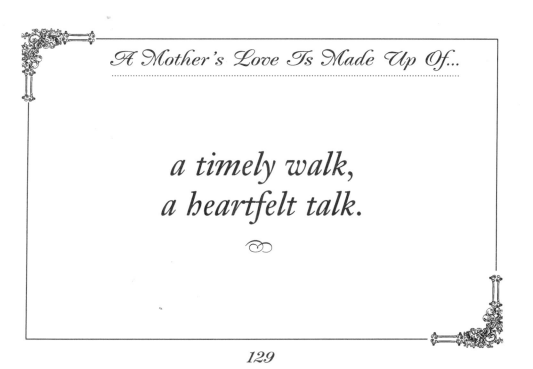

A Mother's Love Is Made Up Of...

a timely walk,
a heartfelt talk.

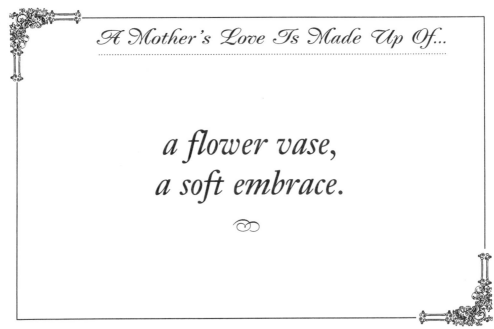

A Mother's Love Is Made Up Of...

a flower vase,
a soft embrace.

*a tall tale told
from days of old.*

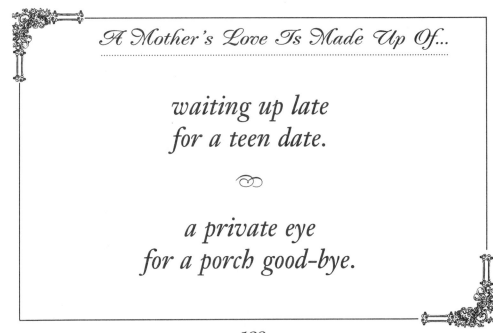

A Mother's Love Is Made Up Of...

*waiting up late
for a teen date.*

*a private eye
for a porch good-bye.*

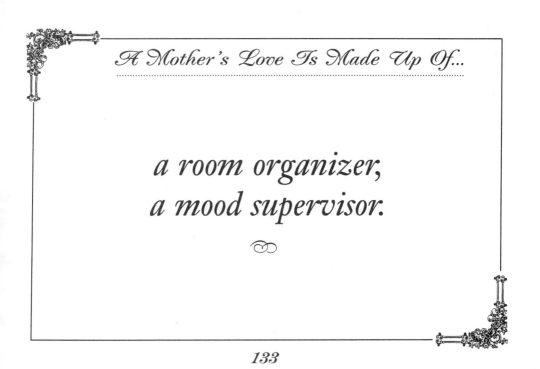

A Mother's Love Is Made Up Of...

a room organizer,
a mood supervisor.

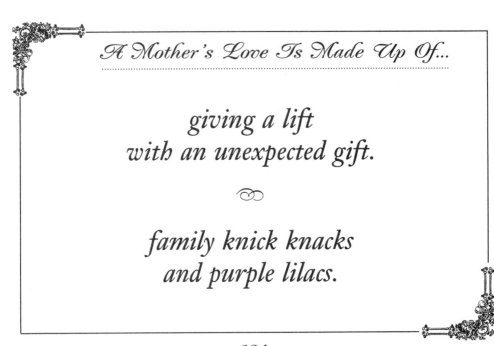

A Mother's Love Is Made Up Of...

giving a lift
with an unexpected gift.

∞

family knick knacks
and purple lilacs.

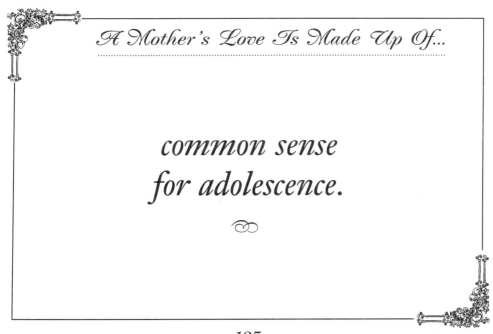

A Mother's Love Is Made Up Of...

**common sense
for adolescence.**

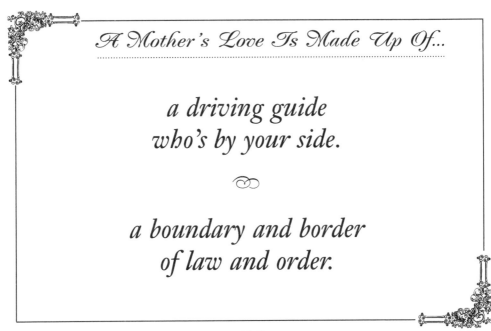

A Mother's Love Is Made Up Of...

*a driving guide
who's by your side.*

∞

*a boundary and border
of law and order.*

a date checker,
a mate selector.

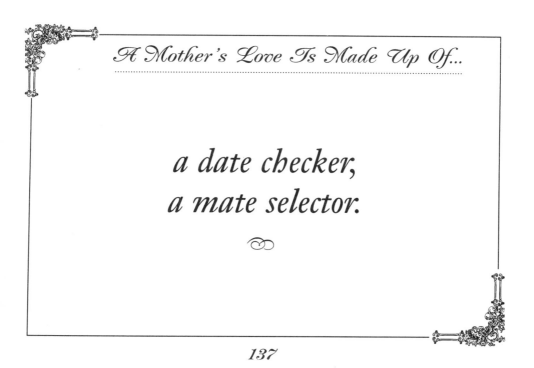

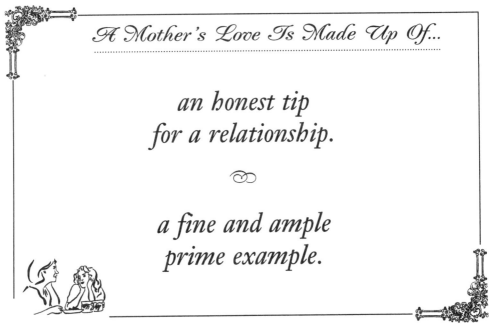

A Mother's Love Is Made Up Of...

*an honest tip
for a relationship.*

*a fine and ample
prime example.*

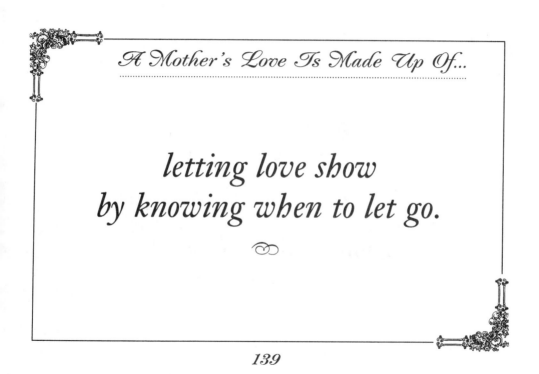

*letting love show
by knowing when to let go.*

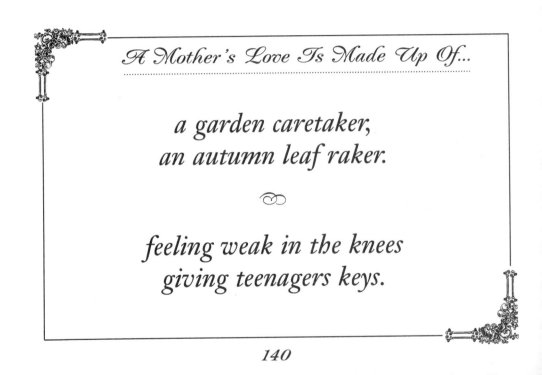

A Mother's Love Is Made Up Of...

a garden caretaker,
an autumn leaf raker.

feeling weak in the knees
giving teenagers keys.

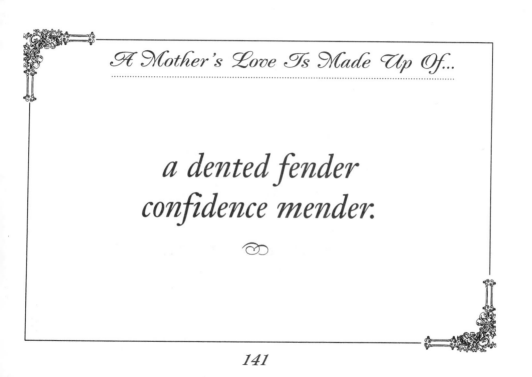

A Mother's Love Is Made Up Of...

*a dented fender
confidence mender.*

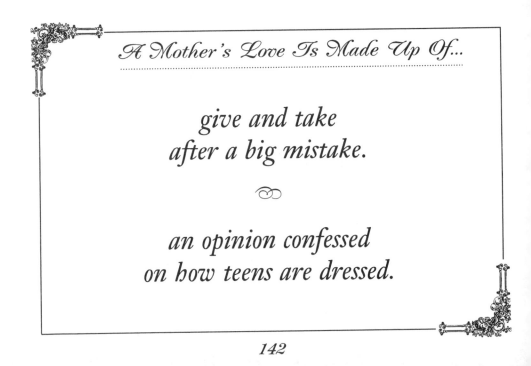

A Mother's Love Is Made Up Of...

*give and take
after a big mistake.*

*an opinion confessed
on how teens are dressed.*

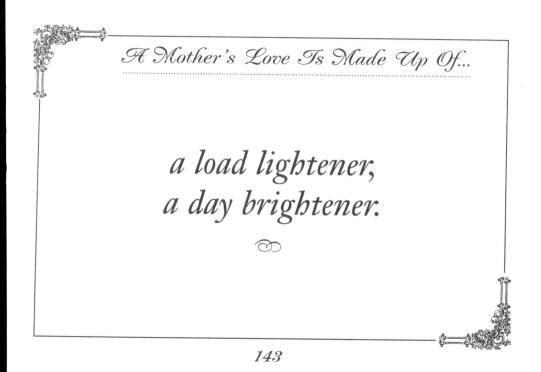

A Mother's Love Is Made Up Of...

a load lightener,
a day brightener.

A Mother's Love Is Made Up Of...

*a scrapbook creation
up through graduation.*

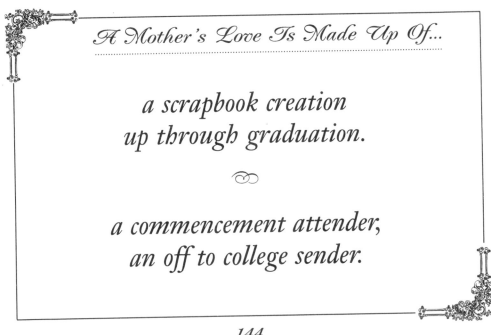

*a commencement attender,
an off to college sender.*

A Mother's Love Is Made Up Of...

*a commentary
before kids marry.*

A Mother's Love Is Made Up Of...

a carriage ride,
a marriage bride.

a tear and a smile
walking down the aisle.

A Mother's Love Is Made Up Of...

*a call on the phone
for an advanced loan.*

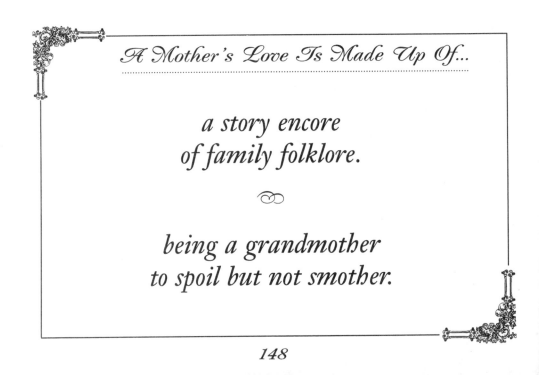

A Mother's Love Is Made Up Of...

*a story encore
of family folklore.*

*being a grandmother
to spoil but not smother.*

A Mother's Love Is Made Up Of...

a hand to hold,
a heart of gold.

A Mother's Love Is Made Up Of...

*believing in a dream,
building self-esteem.*

A Mother's Love Is Made Up Of...

a hope chest,
an empty nest.

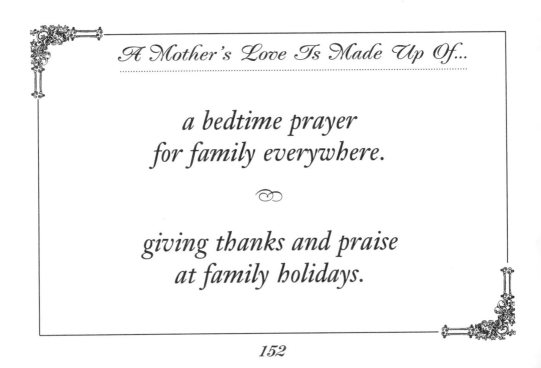

A Mother's Love Is Made Up Of...

*a bedtime prayer
for family everywhere.*

*giving thanks and praise
at family holidays.*

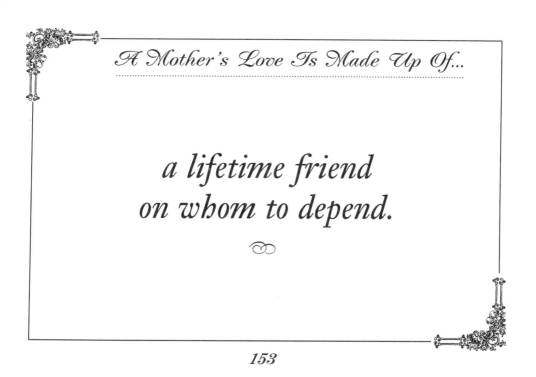

A Mother's Love Is Made Up Of...

*a lifetime friend
on whom to depend.*

A TALE TO KNOW BY CYRANO

The Inspiration Behind A Legend In His Own Rhyme

Let me share with you a tale of inspiration and betrayal,
a story of poetic word, of my great, great granddad Cyrano de Bergerac.
For he had a tender heart and his nose was a work of art,
as a poet the part he played was that of a romantic serenade.
While another man spoke his prose, granddad hid behind his nose,
as the maiden was swayed by the rhyme of his friend's charade.
Generations later I found out about this hoax behind his snout,
and as a youth I felt betrayed by his phony masquerade.

I became ashamed of this mimicry and the heritage of my family,
but then one day I read by chance, the words he used for romance.
It was then when my heart realized the legacy of my family ties.
I saw him in a new light. My heart was touched, and now I write.
The prose composed from my pen, I propose as a new trend . . .
poetic proverbs known as *Rhymeos*™, by the Show-It Poet™ Cyrano,
Rearranged along this path of fame, was my granddad's last name,
no longer am I called de Bergerac; I am *Cyrano De Words-u-lac*.
If you find your lines are few, the words you lack I'll choose for you.
For I've pledged to become over time . . . a legend in my own rhyme.

WHO IS CYRANO?

a literary
dignitary
a word weaver
Rhymeo™ retriever
a prolific writer
and poetic reciter
among supermen
of the fountain pen

Cyrano De Words-u-lac
is the combined pen name of brothers
Dr. Dan the Man and Dave the Wave Davidson
PARTNERS IN RHYME

**More Rhymeo™ Titles by Cyrano De Words-u-lac
are available at your local bookstore.**

Diamond Dreams

If I Could Live My Life Again

Home & Heart Improvement For Men

It's Time Again To Skip A Birthday When . . .

If you have a Rhymeo™ for Cyrano
send what you've penned to the
Quill Guild ™
for Rhymeo™ Writers, Readers & Friends of Cyrano
Write or call Cyrano to receive a FREE
Quill Guild™ Rhymeo™ newsletter or for information
on the Life Story Inventory™, Grand Plow Plan™,
and **Diamond Dream workshops;**
Rhymeo Ink   P.O. Box 1416   Salem , VA 24153
CompuServe - **71175,1035**   *Prodigy - GCSU92A*
America Online - **rhymeo**   *E-mail -* **rhymeo@aol.com**
phone (540) 989-0592   fax (540) 989-6176
1 8 0 0   4 R H Y M E O
visit the Rhymeo™ by Cyrano web site on the Internet
http://www.rhymeo.com